Mandy.

"He who watches
over you
never slumbers
nor sleeps."

Psalm 121

With love.

Your friend
Bohmann

January 2008

P.S. be sure to find the
baby quilts for all
the little squirrels...... even the goldfish.

"He who watches
over you never
slumbers nor sleeps."

Psalm 121

Other Bestmann/Bunnell books:
"Plant Your Dreams, My Child"
"Nana, Will You Write Me From Heaven?"
"The Only True Incredible Me!"

Copyright © 1996
Nancy Bestmann and Gini Bunnell
Reprinted 1999

Printed and Bound in Mexico

College Press Publishing Company
Joplin, Missouri
International Standard Book Number: 0-89900-664-7

Where Does God Sleep, Momma?

by
Nancy Bestmann

illustrated by
Gini Bunnell

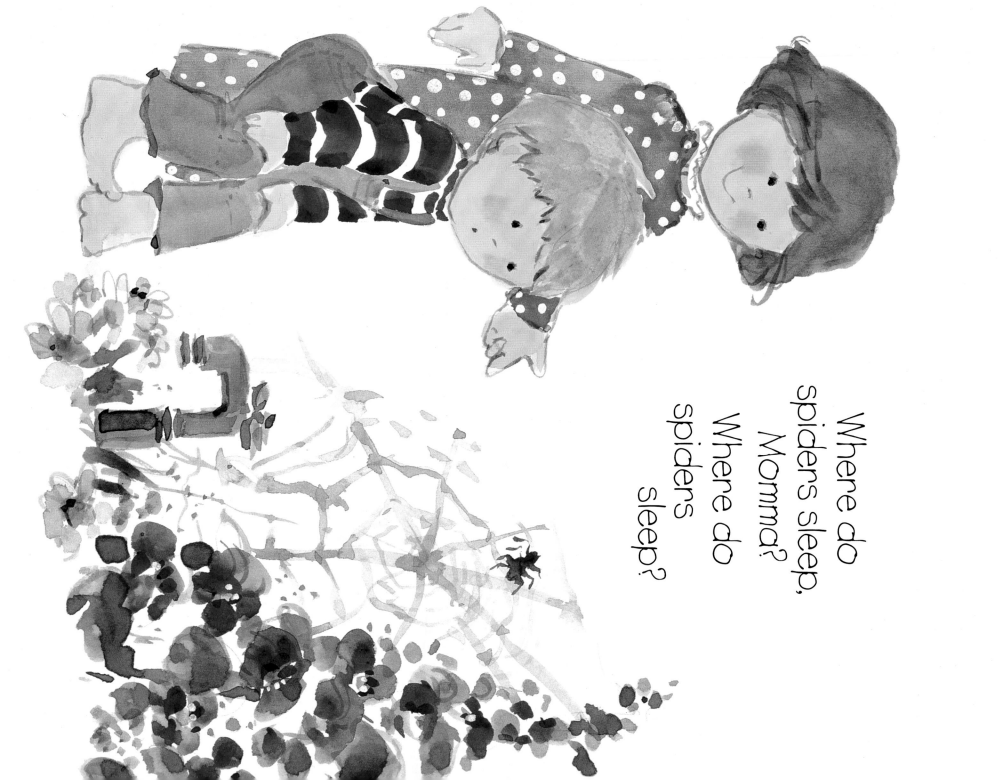

Where do
spiders sleep,
Momma?
Where do
spiders
sleep?

In soft little
spider beds,

That's where spiders sleep.

Where do
bluebirds sleep,
Momma?
Where do
bluebirds
sleep?

In soft
little
bluebird
beds,
that's where
bluebirds
sleep.

Where do bunnies sleep,
Momma?
Where do bunnies
sleep?

In soft little bunny beds,
that's where bunnies sleep.

Where do
turtles
sleep,
Momma?

Where
do turtles
sleep?

In
soft little
turtle beds,
that's
where
turtles
sleep.

Where do squirrels
sleep, Momma?
Where do squirrels
sleep?

In soft little
squirrel beds,
that's where
squirrels
sleep.

Momma, where do goldfish sleep?

Where do goldfish sleep?

In soft little
goldfish
beds,
that's where goldfish
sleep.

Where
does
God sleep,
Momma?
Where
does
God
sleep?

Oh dear sweet child
of mine,
God never sleeps.
He watches over
all of us —
Our souls for Him to keep.

To our Heavenly Father for
vision

To Mom and Dad for wings

To Steve for his unconditional love
and support, and

To Mark Steven who asked,
"Where does God sleep, Momma?"

Nancy

· · · · · · · · · · · · · · · · · · ·

For Paige, Quen, Zach, and Zoe.

How grateful I am that God never
sleeps but keeps constant watch over
each precious one of you.

Gini